Learn About Books

D0903152

Animals in Danger

Written by
Bobbie Whitcombe

CHECKERBOARD PRESS

NEW YORK

Many kinds of animal are in danger. If the numbers of any kind of animal get very low it may become extinct. This means there will be none left to have babies so the animal will never be seen again.

People are often to blame for this. They may damage the places where animals live. They hunt and kill some animals. Some farmers shoot **brown bears** to keep them away from their farm animals.

Sometimes people kill animals so they can sell their skins or fur or other parts of their bodies. **Rhinos** are hunted for their horns. Some people think the horn can be made into a medicine.

There are less than 1,000 **giant pandas** left in the world. Pandas live in the bamboo forests of China and eat the young shoots. In years when the bamboo does not grow well, there is not enough for the pandas to eat.

For many years people have hunted the big cats for sport and for their skins.

The **snow leopard** lives in the high mountains of Asia. The colour of its coat helps it hide among the rocks and snow. Hunters kill the snow leopard for its beautiful, thick fur.

Jaguars live in the forests and mountains of central and South America. In some places, the trees are being cut down to clear space for farming. This means there is less land for the wild animals to live and hunt in.

Tigers live in the jungles of India and forests in Asia. They are the largest of the big cats. For many years hunters have killed tigers for sport.

By the year 2000 some of the handsome big cats may have died out. It is sad to think that this is mainly because of people's greed and the trade in fur coats and rugs.

Many monkeys and apes are in danger.
The jungles where they live and find food
are being cleared for building on.

Golden lion tamarins
are tiny monkeys.
Their homes are
being destroyed. They
are also in danger
from people who
collect them and
sell them as pets.

Gorillas are the
largest of the apes.
As the jungles in
Africa are being
cleared, these gentle
animals are losing their homes.

The **orang-utan** is a large red-haired ape.
It lives most of its life in the trees
but its trees are being chopped down.

Indris look like
monkeys but they
are lemurs. They
live on the island
of Madagascar. They
are in great danger
of dying out completely.

Years ago, there were
many **wolves**. But
people killed them
for their fur and
to keep them from
harming farm animals.
Now wolves only live
in wild, mountainous
places, far from people.

People have tamed horses for their own
use for thousands of years. There are
only a few herds of wild horses left in the
world. They are **Mongolian wild horses.**

The **rock wallaby** and **koala** are Australian animals in danger. There are not many of these animals because they struggle to find enough food to survive. At one time they were hunted for their skins but now there are laws to protect them.

ring-tailed rock wallaby   koala and baby

The **giant otter**
lives on fish in
South American rivers.
It is hunted for
its fur.

Manatees live
along the American
coast in rivers and
the sea. They are
killed for meat.

Monk seals are now very rare. Fishermen
kill them because they eat fish. Others
die because their water has become
polluted. Some seal
babies do not survive
because people disturb
their breeding places.

This is
a **blue whale.**
Look how big
it is! For many
years people have
killed whales for
their meat and their
fat, called blubber.
Now there are only
a few hundred blue
whales left. Some
countries have laws
to stop whaling.

These are some reptiles in danger of dying out.

The **gavial** crocodile is found in India. It catches fish with its long narrow snout and sharp teeth. People hunt it for its skin. They take its eggs for food.

Turtles spend most of their lives in water. They are killed for their meat and shells. Their eggs are eaten too.

The **tuatara** lived on earth at the time of the dinosaurs. There are few left because they have been hunted for food.

This is a Fijian **banded iguana.** The forests where these animals live are being cleared. Now there are only a few left.

The San Francisco **garter snake** lives in damp, marshy places. Many of the marshes have been drained to build towns and farms.

Many birds of prey are in danger because they are hunted for sport. People have also destroyed the places where they live.

Look at these large birds. They are **California condors**. Many have been shot by hunters. Now there are only a few pairs left.

The **monkey-eating** eagle is only found in the Philippine islands. The forests where it lives are being destroyed.

Many animals die from swallowing chemicals. Farmers use poisons to kill pests. Factories wash harmful chemicals into seas and rivers. Small animals swallow the poisons. Larger animals eat the small animals and so they too are poisoned. Birds like the **bald eagle** and the **osprey** are in danger because the fish they eat have poison in them.

bald eagle

osprey

Whooping cranes are very rare American birds. They are in danger from hunters. People also drain and dig up the marshes where the cranes live.

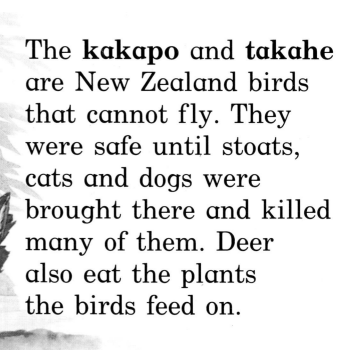

The **kakapo** and **takahe** are New Zealand birds that cannot fly. They were safe until stoats, cats and dogs were brought there and killed many of them. Deer also eat the plants the birds feed on.

These **birds of paradise** are hunted for their beautiful feathers. The males spread out their feathers in a special dance to attract the females.

red plumed bird of paradise

king bird of paradise

The **red iiwi** lives in Hawaii. It feeds on nectar from flowers. People used to hunt it to make a cloak for their chief from its feathers.

The **Queen Alexandra's birdwing** is the largest butterfly in the world. It is as big as this page. There are very few left and it is only found in one part of New Guinea.

This big grasshopper is the **giant weta** of New Zealand. It is becoming extinct because it is eaten by rats.

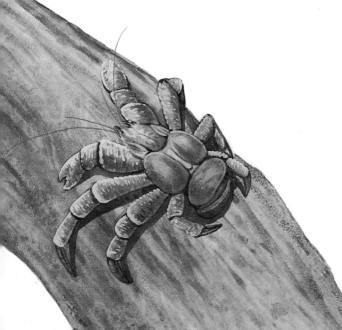

The huge **coconut crab** lives on islands in the Pacific Ocean. It can climb a palm tree and eat the coconuts. People kill it for food.

triton

giant clam

Some shellfish are in danger because people take them for their shells or for food. The **giant clam** shell can be a metre (3 feet) across. Its meat is eaten by people. The shell of the **triton** can be used as a trumpet and is sold to tourists.

The **great raft spider** is nearly as big as your hand. It likes marshy land. Many marshes are drained by farmers. There is now only one marsh in England where it lives.

In this book you have read about many animals in danger. Here are some more. Can you work out why these animals are dying out?

ocelot

woolly spider monkey

everglade kite

alligator